What Can Our Hands Do?

ماذا يمكن أن تفعل أيدينا؟

¿Qué Pueden Hacer Nuestras Manos?

SAMIA SALEH

PAGE PUBLISHING
Conneaut Lake, PA

First originally published by Page Publishing 2024

ISBN 979-8-88793-419-8 (pbk)
ISBN 979-8-88793-420-4 (digital)

Printed in the United States of America

Our hands can touch.

ايدينا يمكنها اللمس.

Nuestras manos pueden tocar.

What do you touch?

ماذا تلمس؟

¿Qué tocás?

Hands can hold so much.

يمكن للأيدي حمل الكثير.

Las manos pueden sostener tanto.

Whose hands do you like to hold?

ايدي من تحب ان تمسك؟

¿De quién es la mano que te gusta sostener?

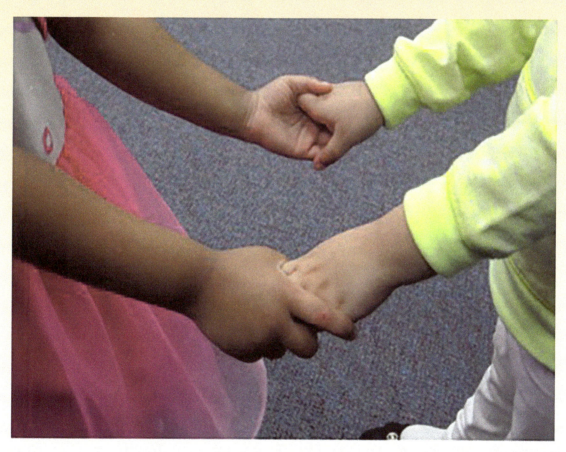

Our hands can protect.

ايدينا يمكنها الحماية.

Nuestras manos pueden proteger.

What do you hide or protect?

ماذا تخفي أو تحمي؟

¿Qué escondes o proteges?

And our hands can direct.

وتستطيع ايدينا التوجيه.

Y nuestras manos pueden dirigir.

What letters do you see?

ما هي الحروف التي تراها؟

¿Qué letras ves?

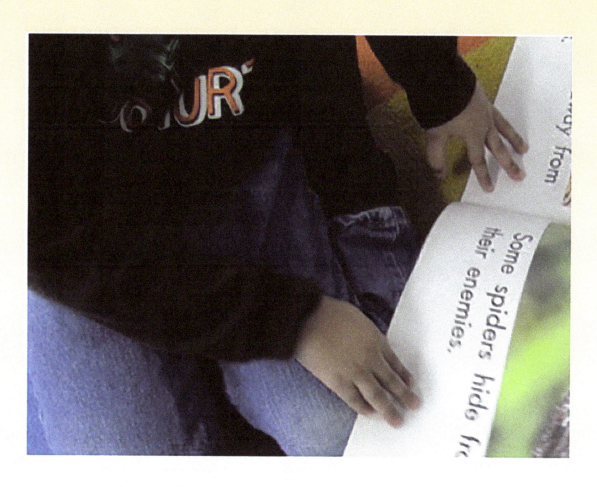

Our hands can clap.

تستطيع ايدينا التصفيق.

Nuestras manos pueden aplaudir.

Can you clap and count?

هل يمكنك التصفيق والعد؟

¿Puedes aplaudir y contar?

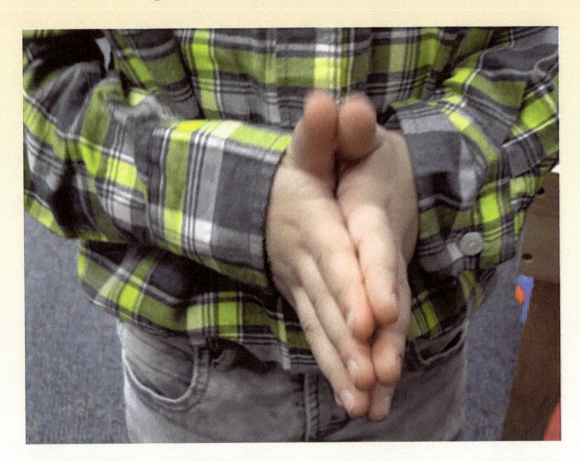

And they can snap.

ويمكنهم الفرقعه بالاصابع.

Y ellas pueden chasquer.

How do we snap?

كيف يمكننا فرقعة اصابعنا؟

¿Cómo chasqueamos?

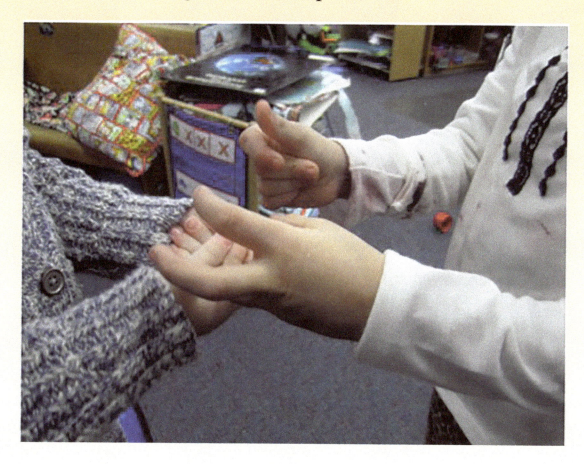

Our hands can fix.

ايدينا يمكنها الإصلاح.

Nuestras manos pueden arreglar.

How do you fix a problem?

كيف تحل مشكله؟

¿Cómo solucionas un problema?

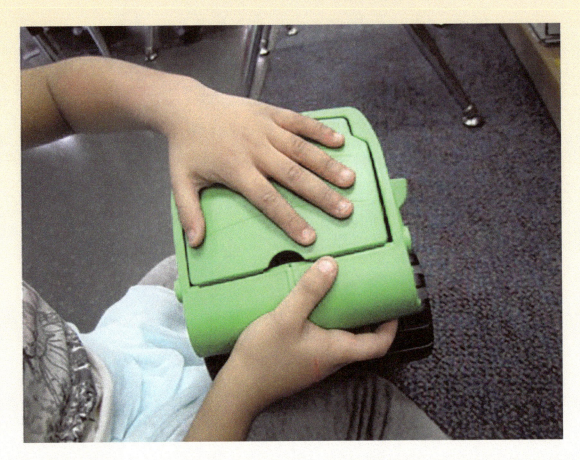

And for sure help us mix.

وبالتأكيد تساعدنا على الخلط.

Y de seguro ayúdanos a mezclar.

What do you like to mix?

ماذا تحب أن تخلط؟

¿Qué te gusta mezclar?

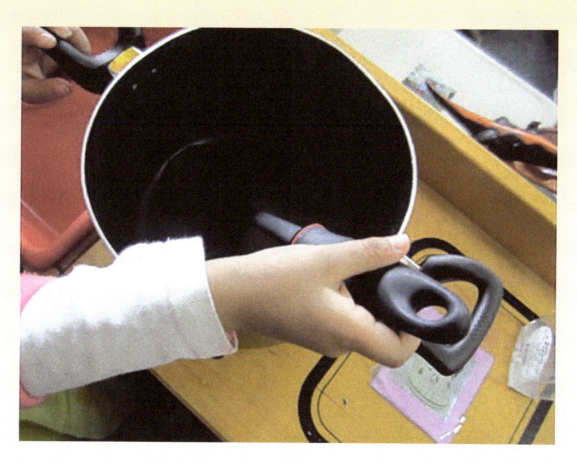

Our hands can help us share.

تستطيع ايدينا مساعدتنا على المشاركة.

Nuestras manos pueden compartir.

What do you want to share?

ماذا تريد ان تشارك؟

¿Qué quieres compartir?

Because we care.

لأننا مهتمون.

Porque nos importa.

Why do we care?

لماذا نهتم؟

¿Por qué nos importa?

Our hands can make.

ايدينا تستطيع الصنع.

Nuestras manos pueden hacer.

What can you make?

ما يمكنك ان تصنع؟

¿Qué puedes hacer tú?

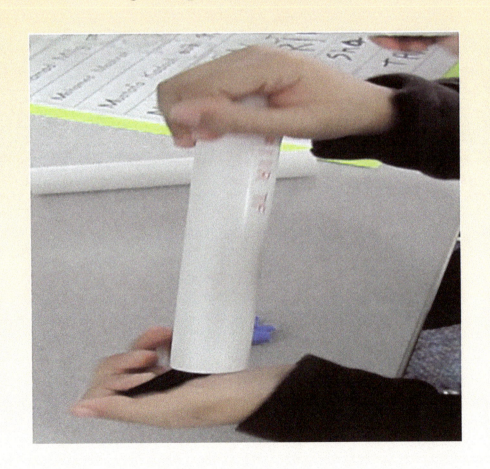

And love to shake.

وتحب ان تُهز.

Y me encanta sacudir.

Can you get something to shake?

هل يمكن إحضار شيء لتهزه؟

¿Puedes conseguir algo para sacudir?

Our hands can build.

يمكن لايدينا البناء.

Nuestras manos pueden construir.

What can you build?

ماذا يمكنك ان تبني؟

¿Qué puedes construir tú?

Every day and rebuild.

وإعادة البناء كل يوم.

Todos los días y reconstruir.

Who do you play with? What do you play with?

مع من تلعب؟ بماذا تلعب ؟

¿Con quién juegas? ¿Con qué juegas?

Our hands can pick.

تستطيع ايدينا التقاط الاشياء.

Nuestras manos pueden elegir.

How many things can you pick?

كم عدد الأشياء التي يمكنك إلتقاطها؟

¿Cuántas cosas puedes elegir?

And help us be or stay healthy and not sick.

تساعدنا ايضاً لنكون اصحاء وليس مرضى.

y nos ayudan a estar sanos y no enfermos.

What do you do to stay healthy?

ماذا تفعل لتبقى صحي؟

¿Qué haces tú para mantenerte sano?

Our hands can write.

ايدينا يمكنها الكتابه.

Nuestras manos pueden escribir.

Can you write your name?

هل تستطيع كتابة اسمك؟

¿Puedes escribir tu nombre?

And pretend what's right.

وا تظاهر بما هو صحيح.

Y pretender lo que es correcto.

What can you pretend to be with your hands?

ماذا يمكنك أن تتظاهر بيديك؟

¿Qué puedes pretender hacer con tus manos?

Our hands can flip.
أيدينا يمكنها ان تقلب.
Nuestras manos pueden voltear.

What's your favorite story? Why?
ما هي قصتك المفضلة؟ و لماذا؟
¿Cuál es tu historia favorita? ¿Por qué?

Turn, twist, clean, and sip.

استدر ولف ونظف واشرب.

Voltee, gire, limpie y beba.

Can you tell and show us how you wash your hands?

هل يمكنك أن تخبرنا وتُرينا كيف تغسل يديك؟

¿Puede decirnos y mostrarnos cómo se lava las manos?

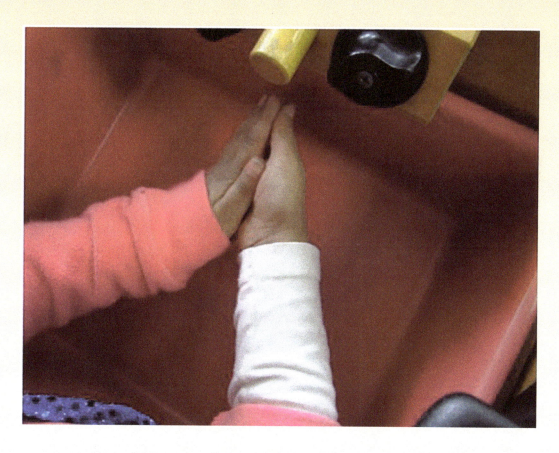

Our hands are unique.
ايدينا لا نظير لها.
Nuestras manos son únicas.

What's special or unique about your hands?
ما هو المميز أو الفريد في يديك؟
¿Qué tienen de especiales o únicas tus manos?

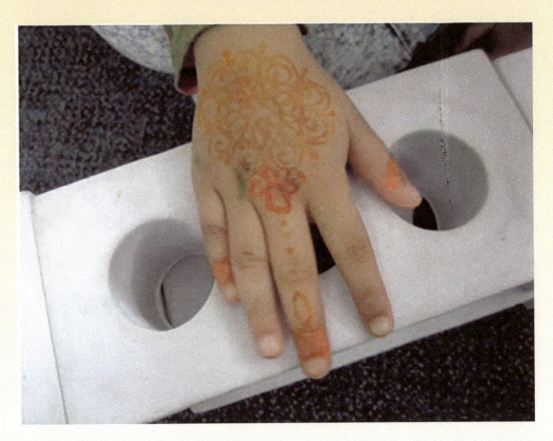

The most expensive world antique!

أغلى أثر في العالم!

¡La antigüedad más especial del mundo!

Hands are special and make us wise.

الايدي مميزه و تجعل منا عباقرة.

Las manos son especiales y nos hacen sabios.

Reading hands are used as eyes.

القراءة بواسطة اليدين تستعمل مثل القراءة بواسطة العينين.

Las manos que leen se usan como ojos.

What is braille? Some people are blind or have low vision. They use their hands on the braille system (with the raised dots) to read and write. Be very kind to your hands and use them with care and respect.

ماهي طريقة برايل؟ البعض يعاني من العمى أو ضعف الرؤية و يستعملون ايديهم مع النقاط البارزة للقراءة والكتابة بطريقة برايل.كن لطيفا جداً مع يديك واستعملهم بعناية و تقدير.

¿Qué es braille? Algunas personas son ciegas o tienen visión baja. Usando sus manos, pueden leer y escribir empleando el sistema braille, compuesto por puntos en relieve. Sea muy amable con sus manos y utilícelas con cuidado y respeto.

At the end, our hands can do and do, but
when together more help is true.

في النهاية ، يمكن لأيدينا أن تفعل و تفعل الكثير، لكن.
عندما تجتمع الايادي تساعد اكثر وهذه حقيقه

Al final, nuestras manos pueden hacer y hacer,
pero cuando están juntas hay más ayuda.

Can you find the hands with the henna? Here are some factual information about henna:

هل يمكنك إيجاد: ايدي منقوشة بالحناء؟ إليك
بعض المعلومات الواقعية عن الحناء:

¿Puedes encontrar las manos con la henna? Aquí hay información objetiva sobre la henna:

- Henna is plant-based dye.
- Henna is used as a temporary body art or hair dye. It can last for a few days to weeks.
- Many people around the world use henna. Henna is used in the Arabian Peninsula and many parts of Africa and Asia. It's been used for many years for special occasions, such as the Eid holidays, weddings, parties, and fun gatherings.
- Henna can be used as long as it's a natural, healthy, organic henna driven from the henna plant; that usually does not have any side effects. The word *henna* can be used in some skin and hair dyes that were not driven from the henna tree that can cause skin reactions.

- الحناء صبغة نباتية.
- تستخدم الحناء كنقش و وشم مؤقت للجسم أو صبغة للشعر يمكن أن يستمر من بضعة أيام إلى أسابيع.
- كثير من الناس حول العالم يستخدمون الحناء. تستخدم الحناء في شبه الجزيرة العربية وأجزاء كثيرة من أفريقيا وآسيا.
- تم استخدامها لسنوات عديدة للمناسبات الخاصة ، مثل عطلة العيد حفلات الزفاف و غيرها والتجمعات الممتعة.
- يمكن استخدام الحناء طالما أنها حناء عضوية صحية طبيعية مستخرجة من نبات الحناء ؛ التي عادة ليس لها أي آثار جانبية.
- يمكن استخدام كلمة الحناء في بعض أصباغ الجلد والشعر التي لم تنزع من شجرة الحناء والتي يمكن أن تسبب تفاعلات جلدية.

- La henna es un tinte a base de plantas.
- La henna se usa como arte corporal temporal o tinte para el cabello. Puede durar de unos pocos días a semanas.
- Muchas personas en todo el mundo usan henna. La henna se usa en la Península Arábiga y en muchas partes de África y Asia. Se ha utilizado durante muchos años para ocasiones especiales, como las festividades de Eid, bodas, fiestas y reuniones divertidas.
- La henna se puede usar siempre que sea una henna orgánica natural y saludable, extraída de la planta de henna; que por lo general no tiene efectos secundarios. La palabra Henna se puede usar en algunos tintes para la piel y el cabello que no provienen del árbol de henna y que pueden causar reacciones en la piel.

#1 Song, Canción, أغنية :

One hand washes the other
Una mano lava la otra
يد تغسل الأخرى

I wash my hands
mis manitos lavo yo
غسلت يدي

with water and soap
con agüita y con jabón
بالماء والصابون

#2 Song, Canción,أغنية
I take out a little hand; I make her dance
Saco una manito la hago bailar
أخرج يدي الصغيرة ،اجعلها ترقص
ترقص

I close it, open it, and save it again
La cierro, la abro y la vuelvo a guardar
اغلقها ،افتحها،واتركها مراراً

I take out another little hand; I make her dance
Saco otra manito la hago bailar
أخرج يدي الصغيرة ،اجعلها ترقص
ترقص

I close it, open it, and save it again
La cierro, la abro y la vuelvo a guardar
اغلقها ،افتحها،واتركها مراراً

(Latin American popular songs)
Canciones populares Latinoamericanas.
(أغنية مشهورة في أمريكا اللاتينية)

Name: _____   Date: _____

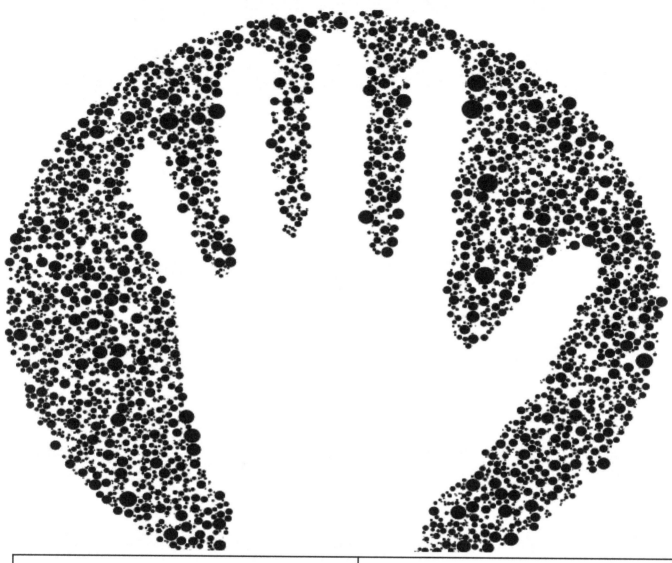

Hold my hands and play with me,	امسك يديَ و العب معي
because my little hands and fingers will grow,	فإن يدي و أناملي الصغيرة ستنمو
and memories will be left to see.	وستبقى الذكرى
Talk to me and enjoy my young voice.	حدثني واستمتع بصوتي الطفولي
We will both grow and remember the times	كلانا سننمو ونتذكر
but not the messy floor with toys.	لكن ليس فوضى الالعاب المتناثره
Paint my hand and place on here,	ألون يدي وأضعها هنا
so we will have a handprint	سيكون لدينا بصمة ايدينا
of my early childhood hand to share.	بفترة الحضانه لنتذكرها
By Samia Saleh	سامية صالح

By:Samia Saleh 2024

About the Author

Samia Saleh is a proud educator in the field of early childhood. She was born in a village in central Yemen. She immigrated to the great USA when she was nine years old. She loves education and has been fighting for the young and old to be educated and supported to reach their goals and dreams. Her journey in the education field was not an easy one, but with her faith, commitment, and resilience, she has met many of her goals and dreams. She is a proud daughter of Said and Sharifa; mother of three young men— Bassam, Hani, and Walid; and wife of Saleh. She loves the world and sharing her expertise and experiences with everyone to support and educate for a better future.

This is the first book that she will publish, and more will be coming in the near future. Her ideas, expertise, experiences, interests, and philosophy will be the guide to her future publications. She focuses on building social, emotional, and communication skills as the core and foundation to a successful experience in everything in life. She will bring ideas into her work from all over the world so that everyone that touches her work will feel represented and loved.

عن المؤلف

سامية صالح معلمة معتمدة في مجال الطفولة المبكرة. ولدت في قرية في وسط اليمن. هاجرت إلى الولايات المتحدة الأمريكية عندما كانت في التاسعة من عمرها. تحب التعليم وتناضل من أجل تعليم الصغار والكبار ودعمهم للوصول إلى أهدافهم وأحلامهم. لم تكن رحلتها في مجال التعليم رحلة سهلة ، ولكن إيمانها والتزامها ومرونتها ، حققت العديد من أهدافها وأحلامها. هي ابنة فخورة لسعيد وشريفة. أم لثلاثة شبان هم بسام وهاني ووليد وزوجة لصالح. إنها تحب العالم وتشارك خبراتها وتجاربها مع الجميع لدعم وتعليم من أجل مستقبل أفضل. هذا هو أول كتاب تصدره ، وسيأتي المزيد في المستقبل القريب. أفكارها ، ستكون الخبرة والتجارب والاهتمامات والفلسفة دليلاً لمنشوراتها المستقبلية. هي تركز على بناء المهارات الاجتماعية والعاطفية والتواصلية كأساس وأساس لتجربة ناجحة في كل شيء في الحياة. سوف تجلب أفكارا إلى عملها من جميع أنحاء العالم حتى يشعر كل من يلمس عملها بأنه جزء من عملها ومرغوب.

Sobre el Autor

Samia Saleh es una orgullosa educadora en el campo de la primera infancia. Nació en un pueblo del centro de Yemen. Emigró a los grandes Estados Unidos cuando tenía nueve años. Le encanta la educación y ha estado luchando para que jóvenes y mayores sean educados y apoyados para alcanzar sus metas y sueños. Su viaje en el campo de la educación no fue fácil, pero con su fe, compromiso y resiliencia, ha cumplido muchas de sus metas y sueños. Es una orgullosa hija de Said y Sharifa; madre de tres jóvenes: Bassam, Hani y Walid; y esposa de Saleh. Ella ama el mundo y comparte sus conocimientos y experiencias con todos para apoyar y educar para un futuro mejor.

Este es el primer libro que publicará, y vendrán más en un futuro cercano. Sus ideas, conocimientos, experiencias, intereses y filosofía serán la guía para sus futuras publicaciones. Ella se enfoca en desarrollar habilidades sociales, emocionales y de comunicación como la base núcleo para una experiencia exitosa en todo en la vida. Ella traerá ideas a su trabajo de todo el mundo para que todo el que toque su obra se sienta representado y querido.

I want to thank my friends Ivana for the Spanish translation and Nabilah for proofreading my Arabic translation.

Please follow and support my YouTube and Instagram channels:

يرجى متابعة ودعم قناتي على:

Siga y acompañe mi canal de YouTube e Instagram:

- https://www.youtube.com/channel/ UCMdP1j5zWpurUnI_G82amgA
- Instagram accounts:
- https://instagram.com/mrs. salehs?igshid=YmMyMTA2M2Y=
- https://www.instagram.com/samias_boutique

Check out my channels. Please follow,
like, and subscribe for updates!
Youtube: @samiasaleh898

Instagram: @samias_boutique

@SAMIAS_BOUTIQUE

Instagram: @mrs.salehs

@MRS.SALEHS

Printed in the USA
CPSIA information can be obtained
at www.ICGtesting.com
CBHW061403250824
13581CB00075B/1662

9 798887 934198